GIRL TALK

FUN WITH FRIENDS

Style Secrets for Girls

STEPHANIE TURNBULL

A+

Smart Apple Media

Published by Smart Apple Media, an imprint of Black Rabbit Books
P.O. Box 3263, Mankato, Minnesota 56002
www.blackrabbitbooks.com

Library of Congress Cataloging-in-
Publication Data

Turnbull, Stephanie.
Fun with friends : style secrets for girls /
by Stephanie Turnbull.
pages cm.—(Girl talk)
Summary: "A fun magazine-like book for preteen and teen girls
on party planning. Includes ideas for themed parties, crafts and games
for entertainment, and recipes for snacks and meals"—Provided by publisher.
Includes index.
ISBN 978-1-59920-946-3 (library binding)—ISBN 978-1-62588-997-3 (ebook)
1. Children's parties—Juvenile literature. 2. Parties—Juvenile literature. 3. Parties—Planning—Juvenile literature.
4. Handicraft for girls—Juvenile literature. 5. Games—Juvenile literature. 6. Cooking—Juvenile literature. 7. Preteens—
Social life and customs—Juvenile literature. 8. Teenage girls—Social life and customs—Juvenile literature. I. Title.
GV1205.T87 2014
793.2'1—dc23
                        2012051571

Created by Appleseed Editions Ltd,
Designed and illustrated by Guy Callaby
Edited by Mary-Jane Wilkins

Picture credits
t = top, b = bottom, l = left, r = right, c = center
title page iStockphoto/Thinkstock; page 2t Sailorr, b Africa Studio/both Shutterstock; 3 Mim Waller; 4c Hemera/
Thinkstock, b Elena Elisseeva/Shutterstock; 5tl kuleczka, tr wacpan, frames tuulijumala, c l to r CREATISTA, iofoto,
Pinkcandy, bl Igor_Kovalchuk/all Shutterstock, r gary yim/Shutterstock.com; 6 Comstock/Thinkstock; 7t Rob Stark/
Shutterstock; 8t Elena Rostunova, cl Eric Wagner, c Dudaeva, r DNF Style, b Monkey Business Images, inset StockLite/all
Shutterstock; 10t Andresr, board background Malgorzata Kistryn/both Shutterstock, celebrities t l to r Featureflash, K2
images, s_bukley, c l to r Christian Bertrand, Helga Esteb, Joe Seer, Mr Pics, b l to r s_bukley, Featureflash, thelefty/all
Shutterstock.com, babies l Lane V.Erickson, r AlexSutula, b artcphotos/all Shutterstock; 11t Filip Fuxa, jigsaw pieces
Tatiana Popova/both Shutterstock, post-its iStockphoto/Thinkstock, cr Oleg Golonev, br Bragin Alexey/Shutterstock;
12t bikeriderlondon, b NinaMalyna; 14 Ingram Publishing/Thinkstock; 15l vita khorzhevska, b Rafael Pacheco/both
Shutterstock; 16t Mara008, c Iwona Grodzka/both Shutterstock; 17 Mim Waller; 18t Kotomiti Okuma/Shutterstock; 19t
Eternalfeelings, bl Lena Ivanova, br Andrei Kuzmik; 20 Anatoliy Samara/Shutterstock; 21l Iakov Filimonov, c Sony Ho/
both Shutterstock; 22t Monkey Business Images, b DNF Style/both Shutterstock; 23c c.byatt-norman, bl Robyn
Mackenzie/both Shutterstock; 24tr Galina Barskaya, l t to b aquariagirl1970, Bogdan Shahanski, Elena Elisseeva, Teresa
Kasprzycka, Anna Hoychuk/all Shutterstock; 26t alexkatkov/Shutterstock; 27tr carlosdelacalle, bl Robyn
Mackenzie, br stockcreations; 28 iStockphoto/Thinkstock; 29t Ingram Publishing/Thinkstock, r
Laura Maeva, bl Pressmaster, br Hong Vo/all Shutterstock; 30t infografick, b
Afonkin_Y/both Shutterstock; 31 Jiri Hera/Shutterstock; 32 iStockphoto/
Thinkstock
Front cover: Darrin Henry/Shutterstock

Printed in the United States at Corporate Graphics
in North Mankato, Minnesota.
PODAD5005
052013

9 8 7 6 5 4 3 2 1

Contents

Let's Get Together

Spending time with friends is a fantastic way to relax and enjoy yourself. Whether there are just two of you or a great big gang, there are all kinds of activities to do together—some quiet and calm, others crazy and creative. You and your friends will never be bored again!

Pssst... Hot Tip!
Look out for these tips throughout the book. They give you lots of hints and advice for planning amazing activities with friends.

It doesn't matter how many friends you have—it's how good they are that counts.

Celebrate!

Birthday parties are a perfect time to have fun with friends, but you could also have a Halloween or Christmas party, an end of term or post-exam party, or even a party just to liven up a boring month!

Mia telling one of her totally crazy stories

Shelley "helping" me with my homework

Zoey and Emily rocking the karaoke machine

Parties are fun, but don't forget all the other times when friends are great company.

Fun and Games

A sleepover with a few close friends is a great chance to giggle and gossip. Or how about organizing a picnic or day trip for your friends and their families? If there's a big sporting event or awards show on TV, you could invite friends to watch it, or rent DVDs for a movie night.

Party Time

Girls in **Latin America** traditionally have a big party with dancing to celebrate their 15th birthday.

Masquerade balls, with partygoers wearing masks, were popular in 15th-century Europe.

The world's biggest annual party is the Rio de Janeiro Carnival, a four-day festival attended by millions.

Perfect Planning

Some get-togethers take very little planning. Just meet in the park after school or head to the mall on a Saturday. But bigger parties or sleepovers need preparation. Here are some great planning tips.

Inventing and discussing exciting party or sleepover ideas can be as much fun as the event itself!

Think Smart

Think about what you want to do, and when and where to do it. Get permission from adults, make any bookings, and list everything you'll need, such as food and games. Anticipate problems—for example, could you picnic inside if it rains?

Be a Great Host

Remember, this isn't all about YOU! Invite people who get along and choose activities that everyone likes. Some friends may not enjoy a swimming trip, while others may have already seen a movie you want to watch. Discuss plans with friends to get their feedback.

Pssst... For a sleepover, plan what you'll do in the morning, too. How about a big breakfast and a stack of magazines for everyone to read?

Pizza Party

5 guests max (to fit around kitchen table)

Check if Friday or Saturday best with Mom

Time – 6pm? 6:30?

Will need:
large pizzas, cheddar cheese, extra toppings - mushrooms, ham, peppers, olives...
check what everyone likes!!

Clean Up and Decorate

If the party is in your room, make sure you clean up and there's room for everyone. Create a cozy atmosphere by moving lamps in corners instead of using the main light. Or dig out Christmas lights and drape them everywhere.

Unique Invitations

Written invitations make your party sound special and they are useful for details and reminders, such as bringing a pillow and pjs for a sleepover. Try making these fantastic folding flower invitations.

Reed diffusers smell lovely and are safer than scented candles.

1. *Cut a 3 x 1.5 in. (8 x 4 cm) rectangle of scrap paper. Fold it in half, draw a curved line, cut along it, and unfold. This makes a petal.*

2. *Draw a 3 in. (8 cm) square on cardstock and draw around the petal on each side to make a flower template. Cut it out.*

BIG PIZZA PARTY!

4. *Write the party details on colored paper and glue it in the center of the card.*

5. *Fold down each petal on top of the next, then tuck the last one under the first to seal your invitation. No need for an envelope!*

Use patterned cardstock or decorate it for really funky flowers.

3. *Using the template, cut flowers from colored cardstock. With scissors and a ruler, score along the petal bases and bend them up.*

7

Clever Costumes

Costume parties get everyone in a great, silly mood! There's no need to buy expensive, fancy outfits. It's more fun to put together your own.

Find a Theme

Think of a theme, but make it easy. How about a Halloween ghost disco with everyone in sheets, or a tasteless fashion night where you all dress in the most crazy outfits you can find? Or name one item that everyone must bring, such as a hat or sunglasses.

How about buying cheap, matching accessories for everyone?

Pssst... Thrift stores are perfect places to find clothes for a costume. Go shopping in a group and you'll have as much fun as at the party!

Sunshine Fun

Indoor beach parties are colorful, cheerful, and easy to dress for. All you need is summery clothes! Try making these hula skirts to wear over shorts.

1. Cut long, thin strips from colorful plastic bags or a paper party tablecloth. Or cut lengths of **raffia, crêpe paper** streamers, or ribbon.

2. Fold a strip in half, loop it over a long piece of string and feed the ends of the strip through the loop.

Pull the ends to make a tight knot.

3. Add lots of strips, trim the ends to the same length, then tie the string around your waist.

Try tying paper or plastic flowers to your outfit and you're all ready to hula!

Creative Hats

Why not make costumes together at the party? You could hand out paper plates and ask everyone to divide them into eight segments, then cut along the lines.

Presto! Instant party hats!

Decorate with stickers, plastic gems, or sequins.

Great Games

Party games aren't just for little kids. They're a great way of keeping a party lively. Have fun with old favorites such as musical chairs (or musical sleeping bags at a sleepover) or try these ideas.

Board games can keep you busy for hours. Just don't get too competitive!

Photo Fun

Before the party, create a collage of celebrities cut from magazines, keeping a list of who they are. See how many famous faces your party guests can name.

Or if you have a lot of guests, ask everyone to bring a photo of themselves as a baby and hand it to you in secret. Lay out the photos and let everyone guess who's who.

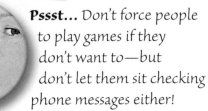

Pssst... Don't force people to play games if they don't want to—but don't let them sit checking phone messages either!

One of the earliest board games was called Senet, invented in Ancient Egypt.

Board Game Challenge

Turn your party into a board game tournament by asking guests to bring their favorite board games. For a cozy night in with one or two friends, tackle a difficult jigsaw puzzle. It's more sociable than watching TV, and you can play music and chat at the same time.

Make Your Own

Why not create a customized board game? Ask everyone to write challenges or penalties on sticky notes.

RUN down stairs and back again

Give us all a HUG then move forward FIVE squares

Don't SPEAK for the rest of the game – GRUNT instead

Reveal a SECRET about yourself

Parlor games are guessing or word games first played at Victorian parties.

Add Start and Finish squares too.

Then lay the squares in a snaking path across the floor with a few blank pieces. Find markers and a die and start playing!

People say that a Chinese board game called Go is the hardest, most complex game ever.

Pamper Parties

Having friends over is a perfect time to treat yourselves—so why not help each other look gorgeous? Ask everyone to bring nail polish, hand creams, or hair accessories and turn your bedroom into a spa or hair salon.

Fruity Face Masks

Face masks refresh your skin, but they're messy so it's good to have help! Make your own mask, using a dollop of thick Greek yogurt. If you have oily skin, mash in a chunk of ripe banana or a few strawberries. For dry skin, mix in a ripe avocado.

1. Wash your face with warm water and soap or **cleanser**. Tie back hair and fasten a towel around your shoulders.

2. Ask a friend to pat the mixture on your face, avoiding the eyes and mouth. Relax and let it harden for 15 minutes. Wash off with warm water, then splash your face with cold water.

Smart Swaps

Ask everyone to bring unwanted jewelry, bags, or clothes and have a swap session. You might find something perfect, and you'll have fun trying everything on.

Pssst... Never swap used makeup or lip balms as it's very **unhygienic**.

Amazing Massage

This simple hand massage is really relaxing at the end of a long day! Wash your hands first and always be gentle when massaging.

1. *With your friend sitting relaxed, take one hand and make lots of little circular strokes with your thumbs, up to the wrist and down to the fingers.*

Use a bit of hand lotion if you like.

2. *Now run your thumbs slowly but firmly down the hand and between the fingers. Do this a few times.*

3. *Turn over the hand and make more circular thumb strokes all over the palm.*

4. *Turn the hand again and make circular strokes down each finger, squeezing as you go.*

Cool Camping

If the weather's good and you have a backyard, a sleepover in a tent can be fun. Stock up on food, games, flashlights, warm clothing, and lots of bedding. You can always go inside if it gets chilly!

Shadowy Shapes

Use flashlights to make funny shadows on the tent. Here are a couple to start you off.

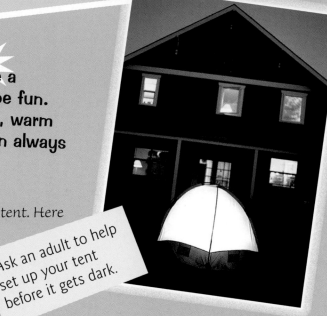

For a simple dog shape, hold up your left hand like this.

Ask an adult to help set up your tent before it gets dark.

For an elegant swan, bend your right wrist and arch over your fingers to make the head and neck. Hold up your left hand to make the swan's wing feathers.

Bend in the fingers of your right hand and hold it in front of your left hand. Move your little finger up and down to make your dog bark.

Look Up!

Gazing at the stars on a clear night can be breathtaking. Try a little astronomy by looking to the north for a very bright star called the North Star. Use a compass or map to find north.

To check you've got the right one, look for a nearby group of seven stars in a long-handled cup shape. The North Star lines up with the last two stars of the cup.

This is the Big Dipper **constellation**.
Its position in the sky varies as the Earth moves.

North Star

Keep quiet and try to spot nighttime wildlife. You may see cats, bats, or even a raccoon.

Pssst... Try to be considerate when camping. Don't wake the neighbors with late night shrieks and loud laughter.

Amazing Space

In a really dark place, you can see as many as 2,000 stars. City **light pollution** makes it hard to see very many stars.

A few really bright stars are actually planets.

Look for dark patches on the Moon. They are vast areas of solid lava from ancient volcanic eruptions.

Creative Crafts

Why not spend a rainy afternoon making cool stuff with a friend? You could make jewelry from **salt dough** or decorate plain wooden photo frames with glued-on sequins and buttons. Here are some more easy ideas.

Use yarn, buttons, and thread to turn old socks into cute or funny puppets.

Design Ideas

Buy a set of **fabric pens** and ask friends to bring an old T-shirt, baseball cap, or pair of canvas shoes to doodle on. Sketch designs on paper first, then copy them on to the fabric. For a sleepover, decorate plain pillowcases to sleep on later.

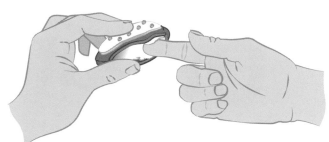

Simple Sewing

If you want an easy sewing project to do with a friend, try these **felt** cookies. Chat as you work and you'll soon make a plateful!

1. Draw around a cookie cutter on brown felt and cut out the shape. Then make a smaller circle of white felt for icing.

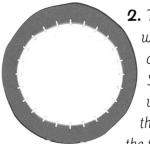

2. Thread a needle with white thread and tie a knot at the end. Sew the circles together with neat stitches around the white circle, then knot the thread on the back.

3. Attach tiny beads to look like sprinkles. Secure each one with a single stitch.

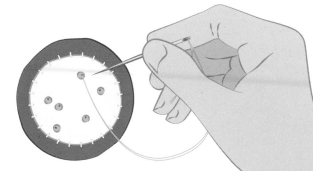

4. Cut another brown circle and sew it to the first, securing the edges with small stitches of brown thread. When you've sewn most of the way around, shove in some cotton stuffing, then sew the rest.

5. Make more cookies in other shapes or colors, with different toppings. Attach ribbon to hang them up, or pin them onto bags or pillows.

Bedroom Makeover

If you're feeling really creative, why not ask friends to help you rearrange the furniture and give your room a new look? You could even paint the walls—with an adult to supervise, of course.

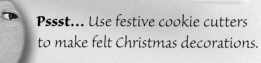

Pssst... Use festive cookie cutters to make felt Christmas decorations.

Origami Ideas

If you're looking for a craft skill that's cheap and mess free, **origami** is perfect. Try these simple designs to decorate book covers or cards—or write secret messages to each other under the flaps!

Pssst... Don't buy special origami paper. Use squares of ordinary colored paper or thick gift wrap.

Cats and Dogs

You can make almost any animal from origami, but cat and dog faces are the easiest. Try extra-large versions to create masks!

1. *Fold a square of paper in half, from corner to corner.*

3. *To make a cat, fold in the two sides about half way, using the crease as a guide.*

5. *Turn over and draw on a face.*

For a dog, follow steps 1 and 2, but at step 3 make the ears using smaller side folds...

... then turn the shape around and fold up the point for the nose. Draw on a face.

2. *Fold in half again and unfold to leave a crease.*

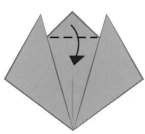

4. *Fold down the top point.*

Sweet Hearts

These dainty hearts only take a minute. Make them in different sizes and experiment with colors and decorations like glitter.

1. *Fold the paper in half, corner to corner, then in half the other way, like this.*

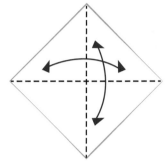

2. *Fold the top point into the center, using the creases as guides.*

3. *Fold the bottom point to the top.*

4. *Fold the ends into the middle.*

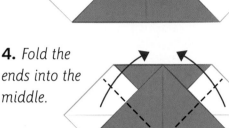

5. *Turn over the heart and fold in the side and top points. Turn back and you're done!*

Use patterned wrapping paper to create bold designs.

Out and About

Don't sit inside with friends on a sunny day. Have some fun and get outdoors! Go to the park, take a walk, or play with bats and balls in the yard. If you're short on space, skip rope or hula hoop on a quiet sidewalk or driveway.

Pssst... Check with an adult before heading off anywhere, and be aware of traffic and other people.

Remember to use sunblock and keep cool if the weather is hot and sunny.

Homemade Games

Make bowling pins by weighting plastic bottles with stones or sand, then try to knock them down with a tennis ball. Or fill a bottle with water and place it in an open space. Everyone hides except for a catcher, who tries to find and tag people before they reach the bottle and kick it over!

Get into Gardening

Gardening is good exercise and easier to do in a group than alone. Get permission to turn a bare patch of ground into a vegetable plot or flower bed. Dig up the soil, removing any weeds and grass, then plant seeds and water them well.

Wildlife Hotels

Help the animals in your garden by building them a hotel! Choose a shady, damp spot and use natural or recycled materials to create shelters for animals such as insects, frogs, toads, and hedgehogs.

1. *Start with a few bricks or flowerpots and lay a plank, board, or log on top.*

2. *Add more layers and fill each one with dead leaves, twigs, woodchips, sand, pine cones, or gravel.*

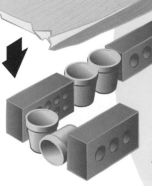

Bricks with holes give insects good hiding places.

Smart Thinking

Why not help outdoors and earn a little pocket money too? Do chores at each other's houses such as washing cars, walking dogs, and weeding. Split all money equally, or pool it and buy something to share such as books or a DVD.

Food Fun

Whether you're having a huge party or a quiet get-together, sooner or later you're going to be hungry! Here are some ideas to help you decide what to eat.

Light Bites

For a sleepover or movie night, you may only need snacks such as nuts and chips. Ask everyone to bring something and serve it in big bowls for sharing. Spread out a blanket and pillows or beanbags to lounge on.

Dinner Time

Sit-down meals are cozy and sociable as you can all gather around the table to chat as you eat. Ask an adult to order take-out food or help you prepare something simple such as baked potatoes, pizzas, or a big pot of soup.

Pack sandwiches, fruit, and drinks for an easy picnic in the park.

Posh Tea Parties

If cooking dinner seems like hard work, why not hold a tea party? Search thrift stores for pretty china, such as teapots, cups, saucers, plates, and so on. Don't worry if they don't match. It's fun to mix colors and patterns.

A small vase of flowers makes a stylish centerpiece.

Decorate your table with an ironed tablecloth or placemats. Lay paper napkins at each place setting, or fold them into origami hearts (see page 19).

JESS

You could set out place cards so everyone knows where to sit.

Serve dainty cakes, cookies, or sandwiches, and offer juice or homemade fruit **smoothies** if you don't like tea.

Pssst.... Whatever you eat, don't leave a mess, or it may be the last time you're allowed to have friends over for food!

Table Manners

In Japan, it's polite to slurp noodle soup to show you enjoy it.

In Russia, guests leave some food on their plate to show they've had enough.

In China, it's very rude to wave or point chopsticks at people.

Smart Snacks

Party food is great for nibbling on, but avoid too many salty or greasy snacks. Serve healthier options, such as plain popcorn or crunchy vegetables with yogurt dips. Here are some stylish snack ideas to impress your friends.

Super Sandwiches

Bite-sized sandwiches make perfect finger food. Find out people's favorite fillings and whether they have food **allergies**. Shape sandwiches with cookie cutters, or add an extra layer then cut into small, stacked squares. Try using pita pockets, or spread fillings on **tortillas**, then roll and slice them into circles.

Decorate snacks with fresh garnishes such as olives, cherry tomatoes, vegetable slices, and herbs.

Garlic Herb Bread

Homemade garlic bread is easy to make and can be healthier than store-bought stuff.

You will need:
- ♥ 4 ciabatta rolls
- ♥ 3 cloves crushed garlic
- ♥ 1½ Tbsp (22 mL) butter
- ♥ 3 Tbsp (45 mL) olive oil
- ♥ small handful chopped flat-leaf parsley
- ♥ small handful chopped basil leaves

1. Preheat the oven to 400 °F (200 °C). Chop the butter into a bowl, then add the garlic, oil, and herbs. Whisk until the butter is liquid.

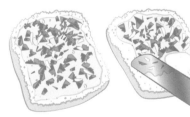

2. Halve each roll, spread the mixture on thickly, then sandwich the halves together, and wrap in foil.

3. Bake for about 10 minutes. Let it cool for a few minutes before opening the foil.

Pssst... Be careful around hot ovens. Ask an adult to help.

Baked Cheese Sticks

It doesn't take long to whip up a batch of these tasty, crunchy cheese sticks.

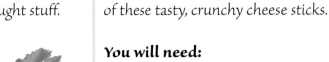

You will need:
- ♥ 1 cup (250 mL) whole wheat flour
- ♥ ¼ cup (60 mL) butter
- ♥ 1 cup (250 mL) grated parmesan cheese
- ♥ 1 egg yolk

1. Preheat the oven to 400 °F (200 °C). Cut the butter into the flour until it looks like breadcrumbs.

2. Add the egg yolk and two-thirds of the cheese, then scrunch the mixture into a ball. Add a few drops of water to make a smooth dough.

3. Sprinkle a little flour on a flat surface and roll out the dough to about ¼ inch (1 cm) thick. Cut it into short strips and lay them on a greased baking tray. Sprinkle with the remaining parmesan.

4. Bake for 8 to 10 minutes or until the strips are golden brown. Let them cool on a wire rack, then dig in!

Sweet Treats

No girls' night in is complete without a few sweet treats. Try plenty of fresh fruit to avoid a sugar overload! Here are some delicious desserts that you can all make together.

Chocolate Fruit Fondue

You will need:

♥ Selection of fruit such as melon, pineapple, kiwi, strawberries
♥ 3 Tbsp (45ml) milk
♥ grated orange **zest** and 2 Tbsp (130 mL) juice
♥ ¾ cup (180 mL) chocolate chunks

1. Chop fruit into large chunks and thread onto wooden skewers or poke with toothpicks.

2. To make a chocolate and orange dip, heat the milk and orange zest in a small pan.

3. When hot, remove from the heat and add the chocolate, broken into small pieces.

Stir until it melts, then add the fresh orange juice.

4. Serve the dip in a bowl so everyone can dunk in their fruit sticks, or drizzle it over the fruit on plates.

Pssst...
For a decadent treat, dip marshmallows or shortbread cookies in the chocolate sauce.

Party Pancakes

Pancakes don't have to be just for breakfast. They're simple to cook and taste fantastic when warm.

You will need:
- ♥ 1 egg ♥ 1 cup (250 mL) self-rising flour ♥ pinch of salt
- ♥ 1 cup (250 mL) milk ♥ 1 big handful of blueberries
- ♥ butter for frying ♥ selection of toppings, such as maple syrup or yogurt

1. Crack the egg into a large mixing bowl. Add the flour and milk and whisk to a smooth batter. Add a pinch of salt and stir in the blueberries.

2. Melt a pat of butter in a frying pan on medium heat. When it's sizzling, use a ladle or small cup to pour in some batter.

Make two pancakes at once if your pan is big enough.

3. Let each pancake cook for about a minute until the top is bubbly, then carefully turn it over with a spatula to brown the other side. Don't overcook it!

4. Serve with a drizzle of maple syrup and a squeeze of fresh orange, lemon, or lime juice. Or try plain yogurt mixed with honey, mashed banana, and shredded coconut.

Have You Tried...?

Clafoutis: a French dessert of cherries in a thick flan.

Gajar halwa: an Indian pudding with shredded carrots cooked in milk and sugar.

Sinh to bo: a rich avocado and condensed milk smoothie from Vietnam.

Forever Friend

Friendship is more than just getting together. It's about being there for someone—and having someone to depend on. Make friends and do your best to be a good friend in return.

Get Busy

There are plenty of places to make friends outside of school. You could join a weekend or after-school sports club, drama society, or book club. Do something you're passionate about and you may discover like-minded people.

Enjoy doing different activities with different friends.

Give and Take

Close friendships are equal partnerships—you should listen as much as you talk! Don't pick friends who are bossy and domineering, and try to be kind and considerate yourself. Good friends keep secrets, offer advice, and don't gossip behind each other's backs.

Try to imagine how friends feel and help if they're sad.

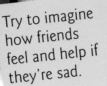

Pssst... Be cautious about making new friends online. Stick to people you've met face to face.

Work at It

Do something nice for a friend today! Bake a cupcake, write a note, or print a photo of the two of you. Keep your eyes open for places to go, things to do, or new activities to try. Don't always wait for others to make suggestions.

Less Is More

You don't need a huge group to be happy. Spending time with just one or two friends can be much more rewarding. And remember it's fine to be alone sometimes. In fact, it can be very relaxing!

Signs of Friendship

Braided friendship bracelets are traditionally worn until they fall apart.

Friendship books are scrapbooks that are passed between friends and filled with photos and messages.

Chrysanthemums are symbols of friendship in Japan.

Glossary

allergies
Extreme sensitivity to something, which can lead to reactions such as sneezing and skin rashes, or sometimes even dizziness or difficulty breathing.

centerpiece
A table decoration, such as flowers, candles, or fruit. Make sure your centerpiece isn't too tall or you won't be able to see each other across the table!

cleanser
A lotion or cream for cleaning your face. Cleanser is gentler on skin than many soaps.

constellation
A group of stars that form a pattern.

crêpe paper
A thick, crinkled type of tissue paper.

fabric pen
A permanent ink pen designed not to fade or wash out of fabric. Be careful not to get it on clothes you don't want decorated!

felt
Fabric made from matted wool. Felt is easy to cut, cheap to buy, and comes in lots of different colors.

Latin America
A large region of Central and South America where Latin-based languages such as Spanish and Portuguese are spoken.

light pollution
Artificial light from street lights and buildings that means the night sky is never completely dark.

origami
The Japanese art of folding paper to make models.

raffia
Thin strips of straw made from the leaves of raffia palm trees. Raffia is often dyed bright colors and used for weaving hats and baskets.

reed diffuser
A container of perfumed oil that soaks into thin sticks (reeds) and spreads its scent into the air.

salt dough
A type of modeling dough. Mix equal amounts of flour and salt with enough water to form a lump of dough, then knead until it's smooth and stretchy. Make shapes, then bake in a cool oven to harden.

score

To draw a groove across cardstock using a scissor blade and a ruler, not pressing so hard as to cut all the way through. It's then easy to fold along the groove.

smoothie

A drink made by liquefying fresh fruit in a blender. You can add crushed ice, honey, milk, or ice cream. Experiment to see what tastes good!

tortilla

A type of thin, flat, round bread, often made with wheat or corn.

unhygienic

Unclean and likely to spread disease or illness.

zest

The outer layer of peel from a lemon, orange, or other citrus fruit. When grating zest, stop when you reach the white layer as this is very bitter.

Smart Sites

www.wikihow.com/Host-a-Sleepover-(Teen-Girls)
Tips and suggestions for hosting the ultimate sleepover.

http://en.origami-club.com
Instructions and animations for making just about any origami model you can imagine.

http://beauty.about.com/od/skinflaws/a/facemasks.htm
All kinds of homemade face masks to test out at a pamper party.

http://cocopreme.hubpages.com/hub/shadowexperimentsandactivitiesforkids
Fascinating shadow experiments and games to try when camping.

www.bbcgoodfood.com/content/recipes/occasions/kids-party/
Lots of delicious party food recipes, from quick snacks to birthday cakes.

www.queen-of-theme-party-games.com/teenage-party-themes.html
A huge range of imaginative party themes, costumes, decorations and activities.

Index